THE MUSIC WE DANCE TO

THE MUSIC WE DANCE TO

Rebecca Seiferle

THE SHEEP MEADOW PRESS
RIVERDALE-ON-HUDSON, NEW YORK

All inquiries and permission requests should be addressed to:
The Sheep Meadow Press
PO Box 1345
Riverdale-on-Hudson, NY 10471

Designed and typeset by Sheep Meadow Press.
Distributed by University Press of New England.

Printed on acid-free paper in the United States. This book meets the guidelines for permanence and durability of the Committee on Production Guidelines for Book Longevity of the Council on Library Resources.

Library of Congress Cataloging-in-Publication Data

Seiferle, Rebecca

    The music we dance to / Rebecca Seiferle
        p.   cm.
    ISBN 1-878818-76-7 (alk. paper)
    I. Title.
    PS3569.E533M87   1999
    811'.54--dc21   99-41100
                                      CIP

Acknowledgments:

Alligator Juniper: "27 November 1992."
Blue Mesa Review: "Great Circle."
Calyx: "Divided Continent."
Global City Review: "The Book Breaks Open."
Harvard Review: "Mother Tongue."
Indiana Review: "The Burning," "Singular Cherubim."
Poetry Porch, The Sonnet Scroll, an internet magazine:
     <<http:world.std.com/~jpwilson/>>: "Broken Crown of Sonnets for My
     Father's Forehead."
Partisan Review: "Welcome to Ithaca."
Prairie Schooner: "The Ditch," and section V of "Broken Crown of Sonnets for
     My Father's Forehead" under the title "Death Rattle."
The Sun: A Magazine of Ideas: "The Harrowing."
The Taos Review: The section "When I imagine these fires burning" under the
     title "Rain Forest."
Wise Women's Web: <<http://www.garden.net/users/wisewomensweb>>
     Danielle Gioseffi, editor: "How to Speak in Babylon."

A section of "Proud Flesh" was included in the Poetry in Motion project in
Santa Fe, Albuquerque, and other New Mexican cities.

"The Music We Dance To" won the Cecil Hemley Award from the Poetry
Society of America.

For my father,

Little by little, we subtract,
Faith and Fallacy from Fact,
The Illusory from the True,
And starve upon the residue.

Arthur Mase Seiferle
October 25, 1923-February 15, 1994.

Exegesis

I've come back from the underworld
for the umpteenth time.
When I was born, my lips
were the color

of Persephone's nipples.
I don't remember how often,
growing up, I convulsed
in Charon's ferry.

What brought me back each time
was the touch of water
streaming through this world.
Born dead,

I was splashed by a baptismal font
to be sent back to the other world
in a state of grace. Instead, I came sputtering
back to this one,

my back arched by the invisible
bolt of the same lightning
that leveled my father
when he was young.

Illuminations, trance, and migraine,
spasms through my skull. Knowing
that I bore his gift, all through childhood,
he was the one

who carried me into the shower,
who held me in the stream of mercy
pouring through this world, and I was
the wooden corpse

flexing in the coffin, the drops pelting
my body to softness, my limbs like cuttings
in a glass of water greening
into root and stem.

I crossed over the threshold, coming
and going, as a snake leaves itself

at intervals in an echo of skin
coiled upon the ground.

Flock of black and white sisters of mercy,
in honor of your kindness, when I left
the hospital and came home, I ate the fish food,
the paper-thin wafers

as if they were a kind of communion
with the other world. Since then, I have gone
walking into the woods, and I have seen death
like a constellation

of ashes at my elbow, my lost
and constant twin, and I understand
the snakes coiled
among the leaves and the budding grasses.

Pressing their tiny ears to the ground
they are listening for that part of themselves that is,
now, forever, crying
in the underworld.

A Broken Crown of Sonnets for My Father's Forehead

1.

When your father's ghost wants to embrace
your infant son, one last time, to bear him
in insubstantial arms, you may acquiesce
and lend the span and feeling of your limbs
to his aery self, consent as his essence
flows into your flesh, or is it a dream
you dream in his chair, the baby coeval
with your father's sadness? He won't wish
to let him go, will begin to home with
ghostly fingers at a spot above your heart.
He'll try to draw you out of your own
fatherly life, like a string on a spool,
a nucleic thread being wound back, all
the way back to the loom of the fathers.

2.

On the loom of the fathers, the sharp smell
of ink made me love the words: my father—
Arthur, Author, on his linotype—all
I knew then, the plaid dresses my mother
sewed, the toy pistols, the paired dolls,
always dark for me, blond for my sister,
the new black and white saddle shoes, the small
charred patties of hamburger, began
in that pungency. As I watched, line
after line poured from the crucible
of the machine, molten as the Milky Way.
But when my father rolled up his sleeves,
I saw the cost, burnt in his skin, a galaxy
of wounds that never formed into words.

3.

Word—that avalanche season at Camp Hale
that the ski troops would soon be sent to war—
made my father immerse his feet in a pail
of dry ice. He spent the rest of the war
fighting for his legs . . . the rest of his life,
at the nail of his one remaining toe,
pruning scar tissue away. As the socket
filled with blood, not tears, I didn't know
if, night after night, he used the pocket
knife to feel again his extremities
or if he was just practicing numbness.
No one was invited into that house:
my father lies there, wearing new shoes,
in a coffin, unworried, resplendent.

4.

Resplendent with this week's lesson,
the self drowning in the lukewarm water
splashed on a baby's forehead, the Father
wonders at Christ's struggle, that figure
on the western wall, as if those hands were
mere illustration of an idea nailed.
He means the final harrowing, the fear
of coming to an end, not the passion
to become, not the fury of the newborn
crying himself awake, his limbs flailing
as he spits up the curds of the undigested
milk and honey. Birth? Death? What is
the difference? The baby is fighting his
way into the body; we agonize the way out.

5.

    Out of world and words, the chant of the monks
seems to unravel one syllable of endless
thread. Since his birth, my son's heard those voices,
male, emerging, low-pitched from their bowels
and from the earth, the way his father sings
along, knitting him to sleep, the sound of bees
humming in a lion's skull, making a sweetness
out of death. That sound is the vein that weaves
within the womb or unknits a dying ear.
It takes forty-nine days to be reborn,
death's unraveling as embryonic
as the spinning of birth. And as we pray,
our only accompaniment, our only
instruments are made of human bone.

6.

Bone clicking beneath the skin, we paused
a moment when our skulls met in a soft
rap, warm, unwrinkled. When my father taught
me, as a baby, to butt heads, our foreheads
tapped together, our eyes open or shut.
Once as he slept on the couch, I ambushed
him, sent crashing all my toddling weight
into his dreaming head. Infuriated,
he never again played, though we kept
cracking heads for years in other, coldly
determined, ways. Now that his forehead's
a chilled dome, I learn the lesson he meant
to teach, tapping our skulls together gently,
kid goats playing in the kingdom of death.

7.

Not in the kingdom of death, in the jar
of my childhood, a male seahorse floated
like debris. Solo, thickening, in a tear
of Morton salt and tap water, he snorkeled
up pink clouds of shrimp, and gave birth to four
children, each a tiny Pegasus, whirring
through a bare and gelid world, circling
his great hippocampus head. Who was I
to fathom such a creature, concoct a sea
within a jar? When I lifted the glass,
the tide of my touch sent him crashing. He
could only drift in the directionless ache,
as his young vanished, one by one, his pouch
filling with nothing but the current itself.

8.

The current itself, his whistling charmed
my mother in the park, an ancient ballad
bearing her away, a melody that called
me into being. Nine months later, propelled
into the light, I nursed to that warbled
sole mio of lip and tongue. But later
in the airless years, our mother would hush
us before he came home. His lungs wheezing
like a broken accordion, he would refuse
to waste his breath on beauty. No wonder
I was surprised this morning, bird song
in the blue ash, wet with wonderful rain,
to hear—so many days dead—my father again—
O Dad, O Arthur—whistling, strolling away.

9.

Away, the baby seems to slip away,
as I ease him into the bath, his limbs
rising to the surface drift uselessly,
until he seems to remember the dim
paddling, his legs all frog. Just days
out, what does he remember of the womb?
His limbs drum the waters, as if some joy
knit his fetal dark and he could swim home
in what drowns, still breathe the holy
waters. As he's lapped by these lukewarm
waves, something like ecstasy shines in his eyes.
When bald with age, he lets go of this world,
will it be like this moment—floating free,
buoyed by a memory of deeper depths?

The Visitation

I jump as God flares
toward me, his squat body and wedge-shaped head,
a chunk of living night sky, a fork
of lightning down his back
illuminating his unfurling, ebony foil.
How beautiful his aromatic plumage;
as he tries to haul off the cow's knucklebone
I left out for the dogs, the midnight
on his back shimmers and shakes. Fiercely,
he earthquakes the last morsel of gristle
out of the tiniest fissure
of the bone, while his front feet
grip the flat, lumpy
patella. He's eating a herd
of Holsteins, a Brahma bull,
a spring's calving of Swiss Guernseys:
so great is his appetite, the joint
flips beneath his fury,
flies up and strikes the door.
I've seen a god up close
before—at zoos, in cages of body
and of mind, and once a stranger,
moved by mercy for the captive
and outcast, gave my sister
an aging de-scented pet. "Skunk,"
she called it, but it refused
to answer to the name. All day
it lay in the closet, its overweight,
balding body, a threadbare pillow
among the stuffed toys. At night, galloping
down the hallways, its long curved claws
clacked across the linoleum
with the sound of mindlessness
snapping shut on nothing.
One day we found it dead,
blood leaking from its orifices,
as if the sponge of its body had quietly
filled up and spilled over with sorrow.
But this—scratching at the hinges of my being—
is another kind of creature, trying
to find any way in, fervent
as a lover, surging
toward every scrap of discarded sweetness,
while I press my hushed self
against the glass, barely breathing
as he tapdances and lingers.

Great Circle

As he aged into impassive calm,
strangers thought my father was a Navajo,
but, as a child, I knew he was a buffalo.
That beast with its puzzled stare, bred back
from the edge of extinction, ruminating
among the repetitive flowers, his shoulders
beginning to slump from emphysema,
like, and unlike, a calf's emerging hump.

"The Great Circle," my picture book
called it: on one side of the page, an Indian,
black braids flying behind him,
bow and arrow in hand, urged his pinto on;
on the other, a single buffalo, the muscles
beneath his thick hide rippling
in a stampede of alarm. Cracking
the book's spine as he flattened the pages,
my father drew a grid

over the Indian and the buffalo,
then enlarged each section onto whitewashed
masonite. Painting for the first time,
he was an ancient cartographer
who, mapping a round earth on a flat surface,
blurs the outlines of separate things:
the man's face smudged into sky,
the curly hump extending too far
down the buffalo's right foreleg,
dissolving into grass.

What he caught exactly
was the wound. The blood seeping
around the arrow in the bison's flank, as vivid
and as distant as the scar
on my father's back: long before my birth,
someone tried to rob him; he walked home
with a knife in his torso but only knew it
when he glimpsed the shaft, embedded,
in the mirror. What did I know
of my father? His pain lived
at such a distance, it was an imaginary line

that, circling the globe, dissected the earth
into halves. While he brooded at the window,
his black mood, an injured bull
haunting the edge of his herd, I circled
the house with war cries. Pretending
to be an Indian, I thought we were opposed.
But now, only this painting remains of my father,
I see in the great circle of the Indian and the buffalo,
the way in which my father and I
were divided, and are one.

The Ditch

Your only attachment left to the land is
the dead you have buried upon it:
the white torso of the elegant goat,
the dog who slid into the grave
like water running from your hands.
You began with a dozen peach and apricot trees,
a lilac bush, a bucket for carrying water.
You end with this perplexing scar
of the ditch; never straight enough
for piping water from the well,
filled instead with whatever died—
egg bound hens, rabbits worn out
from breeding, stillborn lambs
and goats, cats caught in fan belts
on winter mornings—all the casualties
of daily life which you buried in the ditch,
filling its ragged gash, death by death
until, closed up again with earth,
it became another kind of river,
clotted with bones and flowing
from the roots of that distant juniper tree
to the doorstep of your house.

No Earthly Locale

Not far from where Paul Celan drowned
by throwing himself into the Seine,
not far from where the heart
of Jeanne d'Arc was cast into the river
because it refused to burn, not far from where
the slate grey carried away, first, the plagued
villages of the Dark Ages, then, the headless ones
of the Revolution, not far from where
the conquistadors in all their armor drowned
with their horses, fording the ruddy
depths of spring, not far from the Dolores
roiling with stones and sorrow, or the river
churning with lost souls like uprooted trees,
el rio de las animas perdidas, as if this flowing
were another kind of human embodiment, a molecular purgatory,
where the dead are caught up in a transpiring,
evaporating, fluid metempsychosis that erodes
whatever the earth tries to embrace,
whatever longs to hold back. Not far from where
the voices of dead fill every room
of your house with the leaping current
that you hear, amazed, for the first time,
not far from where the multiple names of the gods,
ba, ka, huitzilopochtli, gush together in a babbling
torrent, what flows through you? What is? What can one say
with a mouth full of water? What can one hear
in this unforgiving descent, flooding
the stone spires of the cathedral, drowning
the bridges and arches stained with weather
and exhaust? Each morning what remains
is borne away in tiny rivulets
that dribble or surge through the gutters
or streets, as the city, trying to cleanse itself,
opens its sewers, unbolts the surge of its hydrants,
candy wrappers, sputum, excrement of dogs,
the small change fallen from torn pockets,
all of it purged, running downhill
toward and into this river that collects
as it goes, both the illustrious dead
and that unnamed man or woman who will be dredged
up today, somewhere later, downstream. How will you drink
of these waters, when life tastes so much of death?
No exile lamenting in Babylon, no green willow,
no lyre hung in the branches, I remembered you, O Zion,
and I wept for the unconsumed heart cast into the waters,
for the ear that could not stop hearing
and so leapt into the babbling below.
If the earth has a face, its expression is water.

Singular Cherubim

There is the angel with the pulled-back wing
and the blond, acerbic angel
who believes it has never been maimed.
There is the angel disguised in a flag,
red stars confining its abundant torso,
and the deracinated angel
who cannot stop
swaying back and forth.
There is the white angel of the shattered
eardrum whose speech is broken
by what he has not heard,
and the angel with aphasia
who cannot pronounce the vowels
of her longing.
There is the angel who hums in the beeweed
in the imperfect tenses of the wasp.
There is the angel who walks at the edge
of the highway and inhales deeply the exhaust of every
passing, and the colorless angel who longs to be
free of any blessing. There is the red-haired angel
that curls listening
to the blue vein along your thumb,
and the angel that is rumored
to dance at the feet of wisdom,
and the angel of indefinite distance. And the angel
whose open hand is a living question
and the angel who stumbles along on the one good leg
the frost allowed him to keep. And the angel
who lies down like a dog and lets the wolves
eat the throat out of its body,
and the angel who is so bound by one look
of human recognition
that it returns to us, again and again.
And the angel with the body of an animal
who hides, beneath a wing,
its one human hand
that is inexorably drawing forth
the root of every living thing.

The Burning

If a harrow is a gate made
of timber, hinged
and bolted with iron,
then when Christ harrowed
hell, he broke it open with the same word
with which it has been closed. If a harrow
is a heavy frame constructed by Neolithic farmers,
later refined with Roman iron teeth,
now a modern jaw of steel, in any case
always dragged across the earth
to pulverize and stir air
into the fields, to root up weeds,
then it is like that moment
when in the satisfaction of weeding
my garden, large clumps of rooted bramble
suddenly tearing free of the ground,
that I can come to terms with the fire,
can accept that the flames
couldn't cremate everything
of my father, my uncle, my grandfather, my cousin,
but that the craniums, the thigh bones,
had to be ground by mechanical means,
gears with iron teeth spitting out
the tiny, sticky, clumps into
the bed of ash, so that their flesh
was harrowed like the earth itself,
opened in the act of covering
the furrows with seed as the ashes
were scattered in snow. If a harrow
is a sledge or a hearse then it is both
the blow that breaks open the seed
of the heart, and the husk, the moving vehicle,
the winged helicopter of the maple tree
or the blue ash, the prickly burden
that is borne away. If harrow means denouncing
a person's acts, then the wound
and the exposing of the wound
are one and the same. So in medieval London,
one would cry out, *haro, haro, haro,*
if another intruded upon his house, his field, his orchard,
and not let the cry be interrupted, for fear
the accusation would turn upon oneself.
The outcry, the remedy, were one and the same,

so that the word which means to rob, to spoil, to harry,
means also a kind of rescue, the despoiling of the underworld
itself. So, it is said, in the interval between
crucifixion and resurrection, when he lay in a womb of stone,
his corpse outstretched on the frozen slab, Christ traveled
to limbo, rescued Adam and Eve, gripped each of them by the wrist
and dragged them airward, lurching in the wake of the white flame
of his robe, his torso twisting between
their countervailing weights, dredging
their pale, startled, faces out of the earth,
their mouths, open with astonishment, at seeing the dead—
all the mothers, the fathers—migrating birds
lining up, scraping the sky itself.

Month of the Dead

In the month of the dead, *Lord*
have mercy, the only postcard to arrive
bears a mosaic, pieced
out of the stones of Naples, a grinning
mother of death, in one hand, an empty vase,
in the other, a barren pelvis.
In the month of the dead, *Christ*
have mercy, the first
bowl of soup is never served
to the father for whom the living
clams and oysters were diced
into the broth. In the month of the dead,
Lord have mercy, the walking stick lies down to travel,
buried with the hand that shaped it into being,
a pruned root that will not sprout.
In the month of the dead, on a shrouded pedestal,
the Book of Prayers for the Dead opens,
and the elderly stand in line
to record the names they have survived.
Each tries to replicate the perfect loops,
the tilting *I*'s of childhood's ideal
penmanship, until all the names
clenched in so many palsied grips
seem the serene compositions
of a single hand. Except
for that one name, *Christ*
have mercy, written
in shaky block letters and clotting ink, *only a name*
on page thirty-two, line eight, in the book of the dead.

The Music We Dance To

Winnowed along the earth or whirled along the sky,
Life lives on. It is the lives, the lives, the lives that die.
                                        Lucretius

For instance, the last time I saw my friend
alive—though I didn't know it was the last
time, or I would have said something, put a wedge
in the revolving door, to stop its panes
from breaking up her sandy hair, turning
her reflection out into the New York City street.
But perhaps not, for I have always liked the apocryphal
St. Francis who, asked how he would spend his last day,
answered "keep on hoeing the garden."
So, perhaps, knowingly, I would still have given
Beth the flowers that others had given me—
an over-generous bouquet, mingling the blooms
of summer, and of spring, their conflicting
fragrances, odd lengths of stem, falling over
into the porcelain box full of water.
I didn't know what to do with them; I was leaving
for Seattle and couldn't imagine carrying
that severed field, sloshing, to the other side
of the continent. Beth's arms were empty,
she had helped pick the flowers, was,
in a sense, transporting them back
to their origins, back to the impulse
that had first sent them to me,
and she gathered them up gladly,
maneuvering their fragile coronas
through the narrowness of the glass door.
I don't mean to suggest her going
was anything like Persephone being swept out
of view, the flowers falling back
to earth, dissevered, dying.
It was a real cab she got into,
not the one we invented the night before
to escape a boring crowd. When we talked
about this habit people have of disappearing,
we meant how our chums from college had wanted to go home
too early, though it wasn't to "home," but some hotel
or friend's apartment; we had all been able to meet, precisely,
because we were away from 'home,' had vacated its premises,
assumed a somewhere else, 'behind' or 'ahead' of us—

where we would be awaited with longing,
like those small grains Demeter hoarded
to outlast the winter. In my hotel room, we kept on talking
while I packed. Then, a moment of quiet—like the wound
that uprooting leaves in the earth—began eroding
into canyons, abysmal rifts. Much later,
I was to connect the ease with which she had slipped away
to the cancer, its blood red seed beginning to sprout,
as it must have been possible, so long ago,
to hear the grasses being crushed,
beneath the rim of that black chariot wheel,
as the Lord of the Underworld coasted into view.
I kept packing, cramming everything
into my suitcase—reminded of how Unamuno said
we were all travelers who stuffed whatever
we could into our luggage, then trimmed away what
did not fit—though it was the night itself
that the clock's fluorescent hands were pruning
down to nothing. In the morning, when she ran
toward a cab, pulled away forever from the curb,
I remembered how, in college, we always danced together
to *I Heard It Through The Grapevine,*—the same way
I would hear of her death, called
from a warm bath to the phone,
thinking it was a joke, as the chilling water
dripped and pooled on the floor around me.
The last time I danced with her,
we were holding hands, twenty of so of us,
in a line of bodies, whirling through a darkened student union,
the Charlie Chaplin movie flickering
on the opposite wall, mingling our hands, our faces,
with bits of the tramp's twirling cane, his sad expression.
I followed Beth's white blouse, an ordinary white blouse,
as we rushed ahead, but she didn't pull me along;
it was the momentum of the circle itself, the force
of those leaping bodies, a merry-go-round of flesh, linked
hand to hand to the one before and the one after—a wheel
like that other wheel, black spokes, rim of iron, moving
faster and faster until the velocity, the whip effect
at the end of the line, began to snap us off,
one by one, flying into the darkness.

Cockroach Heaven

When we came home, we were welcomed
by a cockroach peering from a crack
in the solarium. Quickly,
without thinking, I smashed it
and set new traps of poison
for the twitches of my fear.
A day or two later, repotting
a rootbound plant, I saw something
in the wet loam, fluid, darting.
A cockroach, newly born, smaller
than the tip of my pinky, scrambled
out of the upturned earth. Its carapace,
a buffed and radiant gold, it whirled
like a tiny, golden Buddha. What
was I? Who was the cockroach?
O naked face of being, unveiled a moment
before vanishing, forever, into the wall.

The Harrowing

Tethered
to the hospital wall by plastic tubing—
oxygen flowing from the pump hidden within the brick
to the heart breaking within him—
we were already somewhere like purgatory.

In the book of the dead, the dead go on
believing in the body, craving
a cigarette, lapping
with a non-existent tongue
at a stale cup of coffee.

Not knowing what else to do,
I stroked his back as tentatively
as one stretches out a hand
to a stray animal, and he
lowered his head and shuddered,
surrendering to the pull of this life,
as a horse to the bit,
the iron, the captivating grain.

While the living keep trying to open the door
for one who is no longer there,
the one who has died
tries to recognize his own face
in the features of
the corpse. It takes days to realize:

this is myself—a child,
a mother or father, now reflected
in the gaze of a terrible deity,
a human scalp in one hand,
in the other, a seashell
full of blood.

Dismissed, he insisted
on driving himself home,
I stopped at a corner
to see if he was still following,
he stared back, stunned,
from the wrong side of the intersection,
heading the other way . . .
the last time I looked into
my father's living face.

If I had asked him to rest
in such a narrow space, he would have insisted
he could never fit. How can I
walk through this house, step over
and around, when what is now called "the body"
is removed?

Wrapped
in grey paper, a white bow—
the 'gift' is full of his ashes: two pounds.

He lifted his hand
to catch
his own soul
as it flew out of his mouth.
It flew away anyway, leaving
his hand behind, frozen in a clawlike grip.

At night, I wake up and say to no one in particular,
"My father is dead."

How we tried to plumb
the well of his coffin,
saying that face floating in the depths
did not look like his. We covered that chest
with white roses. But we would never
have placed on Dad those chilled
leaves, their cold drops of water.

On his kitchen table,
he wrote to himself, between
the used-car ads and the golfing
tips: "First the soul must pass
through a terrible darkness."

Now I pass through that darkness
everywhere, until the streets, the crowded aisles
of the supermarket, seem transparent,
a membrane, so thinned by friction or need
that a single molecule passes through—harrowed
from one cell, one being, one world
to the next—and everything that is
is whispering:

May he not be afraid, may he enter
the clear light of the void.

May he not be afraid, may he enter
the clear light of the void.

The Crossing

Driving, it seems that I have been driving
cheerfully forward all my life, brimming over
with the busyness of gifts and affections,
happiness, a new red bike crammed in the trunk,

when, suddenly, a car veers toward me,
another brakes, and three lanes of traffic stall
to avoid a deer that lurches across the road.
The animal's already wounded, the right front leg,

snapped below the knee, swings
crazily on a broken hinge,
while the other leg keeps collapsing
beneath the body's weight.

The animal drags itself forward, falls down
then gets up again, its wretched mouth bleating,
toward the curb, the parking
lot, and into a strip mall

where Christmas lights
have transformed
the thicket along the river
into a strangely lit passageway.

In the shopping mall, searching
among the nativity sets—Mary and Joseph
depicted as mice, mouse snouts, mouse eyes,
kneeling before a thumbnail-sized, mouse-eared

Christ—I feel the clear, centreless light of the *bardo*
that dawns in the moments after death.
The crowds suddenly as transparent as moon jellyfish
pulsating on the other side of aquarium glass,

the inner organs of their desires visible
through the thin sleeves
of the flesh,
but it is only the current that fluxes

then empties our cells, a movement
like breathing or a door swinging on its hinge—
I only that motion,
frame, valve, nucleic lock and key.

The Last of the Goat Milk Soap

As the black body of the goddess of mercy
broods over my desk, it's still the Christmas season
when spinning to its furthest reaches, the earth hesitates,
then turns back, the time of the year when I could count
on his presence, extending one hand to test

the strength of my grip against
his, his other arm full of presents.
Like the chocolate pudding he loved to eat on bread,
the gifts were a craving for sweetness, an orphan's way
of measuring: he was a good father when he brought us gifts.

That last Christmas, I had tried carving a cross
from a cottonwood stump and, failing, thought of buying
one at a Christian store, but didn't, knowing my father
would choke on that empty show, that apostolic show
around his neck, and the cross that I tried to carve—

trying to make something emerge from the heartwood—
never cleared the grain, but remained, embedded,
struggling in a vegetable embrace. I know now
that I was trying to hew the crossroads
of his death into a form that could be worn lightly,

as if any child could give that to her father: that X
that I would trace first on my shocked forehead,
then, over and over again, on his,
his face embalmed into a mortician's
idea of exaltation, his hair glittering at his temples.

I never told him how I struggled with the half-emerging form,
the crossed grains of my love for him, or showed him
my nicked hands. He gave me an owl carved of ironwood,
its eyes, all iris, bulging with visions of fearful deities,
its ears pricked toward the night,

and bars of soap. Instead of the overpowering bluegrass—
its musk that always reminded me of Kentucky,
his dream of raising horses gone lame, limping,
his marriage with my mother unraveling down to the last knot,
her teacup orbiting the playroom, thrown

but somehow not breaking, forever spinning,
year after year, around the rim of every rented room,
growing colder, emptier, more absent—
he gave a box of goat milk soap, hand-milled
in Switzerland. Perhaps, he remembered *Seiferle*

meant *little soaps*, or meant to evoke the years
I spent cultivating speckled herds of goats, my hands
strengthening as I stripped the teats of their milk,
or, perhaps, his own lost father mother uncle aunt,
the whole tribe like a herd of russet-coated Toggenbergs

driven out of the alpine valleys by gnats
too small to be visible stinging the tenderest
parts of their bodies, driven by their sense of ripeness—
sweet relief of immigration, hope like cream, new world
like honey—and blended it all into smooth bars

that fit, exactly, in my hand. So tonight
when I take out the last bar of goat milk soap
and toss away the box, its tiny floral coffin flying,
almost gaily, into the trash, I'm glad
I've made my father's gift outlast the year

of his death. For I will scrub even the soles
of my feet with this fragrance.
It is not the scent
of my father—but the lingering
essence of what he gave,

the tripled-milled, handcrafted, lave
of generosity, as when he stood out in the yard
of that coldest Christmas and waved good-bye,
his hand washing the air itself, saying "Forgiveness
. . . Rebecca . . . forgiveness," as I drove away.

Transfiguration

Born-to-the-church, cemented
in it, she said she did not care for
the way Father Howard, every Sunday,
cloaked in Christ's crimson sashayed
across the threshold to the flourish
of those Moorish guitars or swayed
in the aisle to the strumming "And
the Father will Dance."

Transplanted, uncertain,
I should have stood up to her,
defended the mystery of the fathers,
the way that they suddenly erupt,
leaping out of the cave of a book
or the smoldering corner of the couch,
and, without self-consciousness, flinging
their arms open, begin to dance
in the presence of whoever is there,
their own children dismayed as strangers.

How many times in someone's living
room, or my own, have I seen
those mud feet, bear bellies, suddenly
as fluid as water, moving
to a music that they alone
could hear. And if their arms
were empty, then the movements
of their hands and arms created
a partner out of air. For it was always
God they waltzed and turned,
all the fathers, my father among them,
breaking into dance.

The Parable of The Father

Sooner or later, my father would unfold a map
on the kitchen table of every house

we ever rented and ask me "Where?"
gambling a child's faith could locate paradise

among the red interstates and blue rivers. "There"
my finger fell at random on a black dot:

2,000 miles away, Thermopolis, "The World's
Largest Hot Springs," a park with a buffalo herd,

the Wind River and a suspension bridge
that we would tromp across loudly

on our way home every night, trying to scare
not trolls lurking beneath its swaying boards,

but our own fear a hundred feet above the water.
Miles City Montana, Brattleboro Vermont, Lexington

Kentucky, I don't know where my father is.
That last Friday, he seemed the child,

holding his arms out gratefully
to a nurse who lifted him from the gurney,

or, later, crowing in the doctor's office
as a few steps across the room elevated,

temporarily, the oxygen level in his cells.
Since we have cast him to the wind, dispersed

the wealth of his being among the fields.
Spent and starving for air, he lies down among

the animals and the fishes. He who anchored
the maps of the possible and spanned

the roads and rivers with his arms
is lost now, adrift. A face turning

the shade of the hospital walls,
a flimsy blanket around the shoulders, a body

on the bathroom floor, wedged between the pipes,
ashes staining a mountain of snow.

In this world that a week has rendered
as strange, as unknown as the continents

on an azimuthal map viewed from the chilling
altitude of true north, where will I find him?

Lighting candles to the saints, thumbing the flaking
pages of his worn-out King James, reading

aloud *The Tibetan Book of the Dead*, in case he is
confused or lost, it's the same way

that I used to read roadmaps, perched in the front seat
beside him, calling out the miles we had traveled

to guess the hours we had left. I could be a satellite
remotely sensing the planet it orbits, trying to piece

a whole out of his scattered features. Or the child
in that story who is always watching, unclaimed hope

opening its arms within her, for the return
of the prodigal Father.

Lemon Pine

Yesterday,
pressing seeds
into shallow furrows, inoculating
the multi-shaded globes of the peas,
planting the black dust
of the spinach and the mustard, I could hear
the humming of the yellow jackets working the
newly opening buds of the apricots, inches above my
head, and though I knew any sting could cause my death,
I hummed along without fear, glad
for the audible pulse. Yesterday, uprooting
the snags of weeds or lugging away the crumbling stalks
of last year's tomatoes, I could find happiness even in the corpse
of our Christmas tree, scrapped for weeks in the yard, its needles
oxidizing to a rust-colored canker, for I could remember how the tree—
a lemon pine, newly cut down—rushed
up the stairs like the breath of a mountain as we bore it
into the house. When we were children, we followed our father
through white drifts searching for the perfect tree, then dragged
its severed symmetry like a corpse
through the snow, the miles back to our living room.
After a few weeks transpiring, expiring, the tinseled pine
would be hauled away to the dump, where the forest of its origins
reappeared, at the edge of a pit, waiting to be burned. It seemed such
a waste that, for years, I hung my children's photos,
framed in pie dough or fixed to a plastic orb, from the
branches of an artificial tree; each season, we'd reassemble
its fiberglass boughs by the color-coded buttons in its metal trunk.
When the church filled with trees at Advent, I would smell the thick sap oozing
from the severed stumps and remember
how Simone Weil said *we* were all living trees that had to
cut ourselves into crosses, that we must then shoulder and carry,
and how my friend, Kitty, said I was like a tree that last evening
as she leaned on my arm, so I knew as we strolled that final hallway
that she felt that I was rooted here, in a way that she already was not, the white
wing rising out of her mouth, unfurling
her last pinion of colorless flight. Suspended on wires, stumps
clearing the ground, the Christmas trees tiptoed between the living
and the dead, and when we once again brought home a living tree,
a deathly current, detached, radiant,
seemed to pour into the rooms, cascading up the stairway.
Still night after night, sitting on the floor in front of that tree,
I was happy; its towering silence brought my father back to me;
it was the leafy aromatic shape of death itself uprooted and planted in the midst of
my house—so many faces
flowering in those
branches,
each one,
a tiny
dancing
world.

Pigdog

Someday I'll sit down
and sing like the Pigdog
rocked back on its haunches in the desert,
as the pig with which it had grown up
was driven into a trailer, to be carted away.
It was the pig, of course, that went to market,
the hog that just went crazy
trying to get away, its four hundred pounds
huddled in the crawlspace beneath the porch.

Someday I'll sing with the mindless abandon
with which that tiny hairless pup
grew to resemble the pig. How
its canine cells decked themselves out
in the bristling snout of what it loved,
replicating the buzz cut hide, the freckled belly,
while both lapped up the stinking water,
slurped the thin gruel of shorts, slept,
back to back, in a ramshackle pen,
contrived of odds and ends.

Someday I'll have no more beginnings,
I'll kneel on my haunches and sing
with the Pigdog who began howling
as they took the beloved away, throwing
itself against the slats of the empty
pen, keening against the bolted
door of the house, a sound ringing in the shrouds,
baying in the culverts, lamentation
along the irrigation ditches and among the garbage
cans, vociferous, rending the air all that night
and the next and the next and the next

until it shamed us with its stupid devotion,
before collapsing upon the porch, becoming
just another mongrel broken by blows.
I've not written much about love.
I'm still trying to make sense
of the Pigdog. I'm still listening
to the heave of the rasping sides,
to the slab of bacon on the plate,
to the silence chained in the orchard
where the pen in its filth and agony
has been vacant ever since.

Proud Flesh

That is our
shadow falling across
the moon, our motion that we measure
by a declining edge of cratered whiteness.
In the eclipsed light, what we thought to be
a flat disc is revealed as round, as gravid,
and the mind, looking up, thinks: if

it could reach that far, cupping
the weight of that other orb
in an unimaginable palm, it could grasp

what cannot be grasped of earth . . . in moon.

I drove you willingly back
to the hospital, to the pathology lab,

where you could 'reclaim,' 'recover'
the half inch of arthritic joint

the surgeon had carved
from your shoulder. I hoped

for bone with the scrubbed purity
of an O'Keeffe painting

where the antelope that fatally
gored a woman became an antiseptic

rack framing the sky. I imagined
a cow's thigh in our dog's jaws, gnawed free

of any context. But I should have
remembered, in this desert scattered

with the disarticulated, that the bone
in the small plastic packet,

marked with the red sign of contagion,
would still have flesh clinging to it, *your*

flesh. Balancing it in our palms,
our faces seesawing between

sympathy and revulsion, should we
bury it as a part

of your body, or throw it away,
just another scrap of inedible gristle?

It made my head ache, wondering
what to do with that fraction of you, husband,

now a decaying sign
from which we could not look away . . .

> An afterimage
> of the dog we put to sleep
> meets our car in the driveway
> or basks in the sun on the step,
> but only in my mind, frustrated
> that it can no longer glimpse
> what it used to see, rubbing
> against my leg, scratching
> on the door to be let in, lifting
> a warm muzzle hopefully toward me.
> As I get up, again, automatically,
> to call the dead into the house,
> I see it is the mind
> chained, that was always chained
> to the lintel, to the playhouse,
> barking at the distant voices.
> Death, death—I say—what is it?

Testing to see if your suffering
could be pinpointed accurately

enough to be excised
with a surgical knife,

the doctor injected your shoulder
with painkiller, while on the x-ray screen,

the coracoid process loomed
like the beak of an ancient crow

embedded in your flesh. Like anyone else's,
your joint articulates upon a void, so small

half a syringe fills it. As the plunger stalled
in the doctor's hand, you smiled,

as free of pain as any Buddha, but unenlightened,
still uncertain of what nails you here.

Outside the hospital, I killed time
by counting the leaves left on the aspen,
eight on this one, nine on that,
and on a third, only a fragment,
still attached to the branch
and rattling in necessity's light.

As I crossed the parking lot, a fist
of leaves, torn loose, whirled
by the wind, struck me—thassk!
in the middle of my forehead.
I laughed aloud, surprised at such a blow
from a sky that had seemed so full
of nothing.

The nurse attendant kept thrumming
your lips with ice, expecting

the cold to revive you, counting
on the piped-in music, the pinched skin

of your wrist to snap you out of it—
others were already waiting for the cubicle

that pain had wheeled you into. The room itself
divided into many cubicles

by torn veils, the tabernacles
that did nothing to keep us from seeing

each other's suffering. For hours,
nothing could move you.

For hours, you lay dead or in a coma,
for hours, beyond the inducement of my voice,

the affliction
of his jokes. When you finally began coughing

the fog from your lungs, it was his name
you mumbled first, *Robbie, who the hell*

is Robbie, you sputtered, his name,
the phlegm you spit into the bowl,

his name, the first eruption of anger
expelling you back into the world.

> *Roses for the sick and dying, roses*
> *sloshing, wheeled out with you into the hall, roses*
> *in the chill of preservation, roses in the arms*
> *of an orderly, roses imported*
> *in the 1600's to the gardens of Peru,*
> *the thick fragrance of roses filling*
> *the courtyards with the transplanted paradise*
> *of another world. To Garcilaso,*
> *one of the slaves that came with the property,*
> *the fragile blossoms guarded by the prickly*
> *upright stalks must have been an unending burden,*
> *each withering leaf, a promise*
> *of punishment, as he carried*
> *sack after stinking sack of guano.*
> *How terrifying the unknown can be, flowering*
> *in the shapes and colors of wounds . . .*

At night undressing, even the 'dressing'
of the bandage, you can remove everything

but the scar—its red stitch
riding the curve of your shoulder.

The seam is your own skin, sliced open,
then sewn closed,

and the weal rises over
me, into me, paces the room:

> *for hours and hours,*
> *the pain of healing is as great*
> *as the original wound.*

I feared my husband's death in the hospital
waiting with him for tests,

but my father was the dying man I found,
dazed, drifting through the halls,

angrily insisting to the attendants
that he needed to find his way back

to where he had been at the beginning.
While the nurse kept filling

my husband with the cold
insights of barium,

my father kept thumping
into the walls like that balloon

I'd seen tethered to a gravestone
on Valentine's Day. Its red heart shape

thinned out by pressure
and light, it kept trying to pull free

of the thread that leashed it,
knocking on the stone of his death.

> In the dream of the angel
> at the doorway, the world itself
> was a child holding the image
> of the world in her palm, a tiny plum,
> a peach of clouds and continents.
> When I looked up, I saw only the arc
> of one enormous wing branching out
> of the almost human shoulders.
> In the shadow of that sheltering limb,
> I saw that the angel that guards the world
> is enormous, beyond measurement,
> and so could never pass through
> the lintels stained with blood,
> measuring out death, taking
> this life, sparing that one,
> but could only draw back its wing, allowing
> the gold and blue soft feathering dawn
> to try and awake again and again . . .

So I turned to you,
wound and all, bodies

like palms pressed together,
fingers entwined,

on the littoral, labial,
guttural, side of each other,

and the bone of your shoulder
entered my flesh and became a seed,

relentless—for what is more ferocious
than the tree of life with its scaling hooks

and armor, exploding itself
to live on in the drift—a seed

putting forth the tendrils of nerves,
a tiny skull, the lattice of ribs,

the spine unfolding an unfurling
vine, a question floating within,

as our son put on his name and our knowledge,
his heart beginning to beat.

> The drift of the Milky Way
> casting into the dark pools on the other
> side of the horizon, I remembered that once
> those stars were a bridge between
> the land of the living and the dead, a road
> down which the newborn drifted
> toward us. Walking deeper and further
> into the numbness of sleep, I could have been
> drinking of the icy taste
> of forgetfulness, when something brushed
> against my ankle: a hand of water, a grip
> of baby or ghost, tugging, then floating away.
> It was only my own shoelace, trying to work free
> of its eyelet, lashing against my ankle,
> as my shoes, full of water,
> kept trying to rise, to bear me away.
> When I stumbled back to the shore
> after hours immersed in that cold ache,
> the earth itself seemed fluid.

At the Bosque del Apache, we were trying
to find our way back to the still waters,

watching the cattle egret, the blue heron
punctuating the shore, the wood ducks

paddling in pairs, the soft-shelled turtles
sunbathing along the recently scraped banks

of the ditches when splashes in the reeds
drew us to the pond's edge. Something thrashed

in the shallows, fighting the entanglements
of the submerged plants, its finned back slashing

the surface, its head almost visible. River carp,
a throng of them, were bulldozing their way

into the shallows, then snared, almost beached,
surging back to the depths. Not knowing

whether something was coming to an end
or just beginning, I searched the murk

and found only the young for meaning.
Their eyes, a thousand black dots, made visible

their transparent, still-forming flesh, their spines
coiled like question marks in the foliage.

As the water cleared, thousands of the newly hatched
coalesced in a shimmering wave, a form as visible

as a single body, outlined as it was
against the churning and clearing

of the red underlying soil.

> *When I imagine those fires consuming*
> *what has never been named—the Amazonian*
> *"a," "an," "the," all the vanishing*
> *species—I think how in another,*
> *language, the word for "forest"*
> *sounds so much like the word for "world."*
> *And how so often it wasn't until I reached*

an outcropping of stone and sky
where the green limbs of the trees
were the wings of rooted angels
that I could gather the breath
back into my body by saying,
"white birch," "twig," "oak tree."

Just as in some languages, the skies
are named, not for the stars, but for the dark clouds

between them, learning to pray
is learning to die. Sitting so long

at the kitchen table, holding
the hand of the non-existent, her gaze

brushing against your face,
you become so vacant,

so willing to be
enveloped in her murmur,

that when you arise from her, move back
to the knives and the dirty dishes and the warm

cleansing suds, your hip
catches in its socket, refuses

to bear the weight of your self.
Every morning, you walk

as if crippled by an angel, limping back
into this world.

    Someone said that a turkey vulture,
the skinned look of its featherless head,
is a naked skull, a bitter thing,
but once we rescued a fledgling,
grounded by a stray bullet,
and it wore the black and white
headdress of a primitive king.

All summer, I fed that crown of untamed glory,
but its ire was unending as the fire
that consumes what is left

of the dead. Part serpent,
as if something earthen, unrepentant,
had sprouted wings and entered the sky,
it hissed and hissed, so much fury,
so much life in death!

All my life, I have equivocated,
comically comparing the birthmark on my heel

to a small slice of boneless ham
or sadly to a torn pink rooted on the malleolus,

or predictably to a cloud at sunset, fading
or flaring to the vagaries of my circulation.

I have stared at it as long
as my father stared at his wounded

feet, until the mark dissolved
into definition, mere fact or blotch

of membrane. Born dead,
retrieved by forceps

from the living dark,
a caul shrouding my eyes, I

am still trying to read
the future through the veil

of the flesh, by the dim light
of this body.

For I know the birth mark
is an angel. Its infallible

wings, the rushed sweep of its skirt,
the aureoles of its hair, rendered

as clearly as an angel could be drawn,
if sketched in blood on living skin.

Welcome to Ithaca

Since *metaphor* derives from *transferring*
a burden from one to the other, it
was clear, then, from the beginning,
that blood-drenched hall, that it would be easier
to silence pleas for mercy
if heard as the unintelligible
chirping of birds—easier
to string servant girls up like pigeons.
So, Odysseus' heart was a *dog,* its hackles
rising when he saw the women caught up
in the suitors' arms, someone else's pets,
and only in a dream did Penelope weep
for *her* slaughtered geese, their soft white strewn
round the water trough. When Telemachus strung
a wire between two trees and began hanging
the servant women, one by one, noosing
them in a line, the dying women
were described as thrushes spreading their wings,
doves or larks caught in a spring.
They were killed as a flock of birds, as undeserving
of the death of a single human being.
Though, first, in a colder, waking moment, the undisguised
Odysseus ordered the women to remove the corpses
from the great hall, to stack their lovers
in the yard. One cradling each beloved head,
another clutching at the feet,
the women became mere things—
their flesh a rag for scouring the furniture,
trying to scrub clear the appalling
table. Their last task
before being strangled—to dispose
of the earth itself, the blood-soaked floor
that Telemachus meticulously cut out,
so in the future—that narrow corridor
down which so many would be driven—a visitor
would not know she was invited into
a charnel house.

Divided Continent

When I was five or six, my parents took me to a ceremony
of Sioux and Cheyenne dancers. The moving
eagle feathers plucked from living birds,
chest plates quivering with porcupine quills,
the beadwork shimmering
on their waists, wrists, ankles,

all of it began
in the dance itself. A step

that lifted its knee to the waist, whirled around
and screed sideways, arms trembling
with the attached plumage,
the foot drumming sound
from the earth. I wanted to be like them,
to be one of them, so wore everywhere

the red and white solar design of Red Cloud
stitched into a disc of deerskin.

As I ran, screaming war cries
around my parents' house, my hands already
scarred from trying to fashion arrows
from the dwarfed bushes in the suburban yard,
the necklace around my neck
gave me the power of another world,

its red eye, the ruby eye of the grebe
that dives into the water and comes up

on the other side of the lake.
On the other side of the street, in another
lot, three girls in white frilly dresses,
their hair coiled in ringlets and bows, curtsied
around a portable table where real eighths
of a sandwich dressed

each miniature plate, real tea was poured
into tiny play cups, and they, too, were rehearsing

another ideal. I was seven, then,
and, oh my longing to be like her, to be her,
and her longing to be like me—the one

who looked up and stared back
out of the perfectly cultivated
garden of her face.

In school, we took out our scorn and our longing
upon each other,

while the teacher described
our fathers, settlers so driven to own
a deeded plot, a fenced garden,
that they became their own oxen
and pulled their wagons, full of belongings,
across the mountains that divided America.

Then, my family moved and moved and kept moving
and all that lasted was the never-completed history

class that I had to begin over and over again.
By the end of the year,
the threads that held
the beads in place
had worn through, leaving
only the disc of deerhide,

its circle of skin,
rubbed free of any design.

Now, in my own small plot on this continent,
I see in one corner of the snow-covered field,
that photograph: 1892, Wounded Knee,
a red man, spread-eagled, frozen to a wire fence,
his hand snagged on the barbs, stopped
in mid-air, trying to grasp

how white the beeweed is,
its riot of purple replaced

with the intricate architecture of ice;
if it were struck, the plant itself
would shatter. Cold
from all the ways
in which we will never be whole,
after all these years,

running errands among the scattering
of autumn, or driving past the horror

of two horses struck by a speeding car, the white one
with its belly torn, the red one, its skull caved-in,
their legs outstretched, frozen in mid-stride,
as if they were running together,
without explanation or hope, I feel
this other movement

beyond pity, beyond blessing, rising out
of the closed wounds of the earth and the still open
wounds of the rivers.

Birth of The White Buffalo

Each morning, I have slowed to watch
him. Just another 'stone-faced' Navajo
in this worn-out neighborhood, except
instead of laboring over a clogged carburetor

to make a stalled car run, up to his ankles
in unmelting drifts, he cuts a tribe
out of stone. Always the same figures emerge:
a man caped in buffalo horns, a woman

in the hide that she chewed into softness,
both holding a drum in one hand, its taut skin
quieted for the touch of the other;
both sexes, proud of that song

that their lips barely open to sing
because it is the inaudible
song of the body. Yesterday, and again
this morning, he was driven from his yard

by city electricians who interrupted
his work with their working. Perhaps, the fever
to reconnect a neighborhood accustomed to neglect
was drawn by the fear of another

current, flowing from house to house, humming
in the exhausted transformers, illuminating the gardens,
the art galleries, with the extinct but revived light
of the body, a source that others would cluster around,

as I had, trying to penetrate the shrouded sweetness,
to glimpse the emerging form. Just as in the Dakotas,
crowds were gathering around a rickety pen
to view a rare white buffalo calf, finding

in its liquid gaze, the promised
return of Buffalo Woman, undiscouraged
that the curling drift of its snowy coat
was already turning, hair by hair, to the ruddy shades

of the earth.

The Illusory and the True

At first, the color was everywhere, glimpsed
in the tub, dashed in and out of her clothes,
a comic tuft from crotch or armpit, a cosmic
cascading, a blush of original
sin, the cast of the apple eaten in Eden
or the one my father was eating
the first time she saw him
strolling down the street,
or the ruby glow of the pomegranate seed,
the stain of the first blood shed,
the swirl of the firstborn drowning
in the waters, swirling out of sight
down the drain of the world. Oh
my mother's hair was terrifying, fresh
as the flush of her anger, illuminating
the night, intense as the moon choking
in a clot of smoke, pure
as the fallacy that bound me
to her, unable to breathe
or cry out, caught as I was
in the web of her hair. Primary,
cardinal, that color became
her name, the dare
of a nickname snapping
in a stranger's eye, a lure cast
into the depths of a stare, an hour of carnage
emblazoning a battlefield, the flame
that flared on the edge of the cornfield,
the stroke of the sun that felled her
working in the sugar beet fields
where the tubers unearthed from the muddy
rows were the smoldering
shade of her hair. Years later,
glimpsing the brand of her hair burning
in some old photograph, I felt
surrounded by her glory, the constellation
of that hair, its bright faith
ushering me into the hushed
church. Then when? Where?
Leashed, bridled, braided,
she caught it at the back of her head,
its copper tongues beginning to simmer
to the beaten and burnished

shade of the teapot, my father's gift,
the only thing she wanted, rising
to a boil, while the loose ends
kept breaking free, fluttering
at the nape of her neck; split hairs
turning to rust or seed, the hue
of a bruise, the claret of rosehips.
For years, then, my mother's hair
was woven so tightly,
it became illusory, a knot
at the back of her neck
that she could unravel secretly
only at night, while, every day,
it greyed to brickdust
or maple leaves or the sulphurous
cast of a word held back. With her hair
so coiled, so drawn back,
her face became oddly naked,
the body of a bird stripped
of plumage, every vein trembling
with outrage in the high color
of her complexion, all through
those years of marriage,
the rapture of her hair leashed
into a single whip
of suffering. And then, I remember exactly
when she was stepping out of an airplane,
having come home to give my father
the divorce he asked for, she came down
the stairs, stepped onto the runway,
and I saw that she had cut her hair,
the accumulated lengths
of all those years
lying somewhere like dead tongues
coiled on the clipping floor.
Nothing but air around her head, the sweep
of wind against her ears, the short
curls brighter, cut closer to the skull,
so that for a moment, I could glimpse
beneath the artificial highlights
of the permanent, that original
scarlet, that glorious red
still burning in the follicle
and root.

The Catch

We were looking for a paradise, a place
we could return to again and again,
its waters thick with life,
but, four-wheeling into the swamps
of a river's mouth, we were driven away
by the exhausted look of clay banks,
punctured with prop sticks, entangled
with lines, and, lost, veering
among the white joints of pipelines
protruding from the earth.
Finally braking at the edge of a mesa,
burdened with tackle, we scrambled
down an eroding slope and reached
an eddy of a reservoir, its waters,
a thick sulfuric yellow. Two dogs,
baying hell hounds, scoured the other bank,
while we settled onto our haunches and waited,
poised, as if praying, all our energy gathering
at the end of the line. Waited
for a strike, some sign of life,
as the waves slapping against the shore
made our lines go slack, again and again,
until the span of attention went slack in ourselves.
All we caught was a tiny bullhead, the murky gold
of the cove, reeled in, unknowingly,
when my husband retrieved his bait. Having heard
that a fish could absorb a lure into its flesh,
as eventually the knot of stitches
in his own shoulder would supposedly dissolve,
he cut the filament, left that jag of metal
in the back of its throat. Released,
the fish wobbled a moment on the muddy shelf,
then slipped away, its recovery,
as vague, as uncertain as the presence of hope
in those depths where nothing exists but the wound.

Original Darkness

When Dickson fell at the power plant, his body tripped
the breakers, and the lights, six hundred miles away,
flickered, then went out, a human heaven
shorting out, reverting to original darkness.

No one knows why he was off limits, past
the boundary tape. I think he just kept disappearing.
Years ago, I'd spend half of every day hunting him.
Smoking under a stairwell, or in a vacant room—

curtains drawn as if occupied by a paying guest—
watching reruns of *I Love Lucy*—he kept vanishing
from linen closet to linen closet, his face, a buffalo
moon, drifting, indifferently, past the maid carts

being slowly buried under drifts of dirty sheets.
Using a stick to drown the bedding in the churning,
overloaded washers, our lives revolved around the quality
of whiteness. We were measured in the shining

of the porcelain toilets, prisoners of the sparkling sinks,
as the bleach that left its blue shadow in the fabric
first cauterized our fingers, red and white
blurring to one industrial hue.

Dickson couldn't have cared less the day I had to
fire him. Weeks later, he stopped by, said
his aunt had taught him how to cast
a squash blossom in a sand mold,

how to hammer hollow halves of silver into one,
apparently, seamless bead. Each necklace
brought a thousand dollars—he declared to
the unswept parking lot, the souring

stench of the leftover bottles, then turned
and fished a necklace from his car's open window.
He said he had made the beads, languid, glowing
on his palm, so heavy that only a warrior

could wear them, the claw of turquoise at the center,
the size of a bear's hand. I'd seen that crescent before
fluttering in history books, on Moorish flags
conquering Spain or glittering on Spanish armor

as they invaded the New World, worn as wealth
by the Navajo who learned metal-working
from Pueblo people captured as slaves—
each time, the symbol altering as it descended closer

to earth—a crescent moon, a scimitar, a bear's paw.
"Look, if it's genuine, you can't
hurt it," Dickson stabbed the turquoise with a pin,
testing the purity of its blue, a cure

as ancient as Aristotle who said wearing
turquoise would prevent death by accident.
As Dickson hunted my face for some sign
of desire or fear, we both knew

he was only daring me. I could never
possess, he could never afford
to wear that splinter of sky
gripped by a silver claw.

The blossom he forged in the New World
was the pomegranate of the Old, still
opening its silvery, odorless
constellations, seeding

the underworld. Wrought
and refined in fire, it would hang
in a trading post window, throbbing
with light, not life.

27 November 1992

Atahualpa Perez
was dangerous today on his way to school,
he opened his mouth,
and the syllables

were blood, writing
on the wall of a soon-to-be-ruined empire,
streaming down the picturesque, cobbled, streets.
His neighbors heard him whistling

among the teapots and alarm clocks.
Suddenly, the warm tortillas
dropped from their hands, their wrists
chilled, aching, as if handcuffed

behind their backs. In the police station,
Atahualpa couldn't give them what they wanted.
He had the name of that emperor
who was carried by warriors on their shoulders

through the rivers of their own blood,
even when their hands were severed.
He had the name that refused to rise
even when the old world stampeded toward him

on a horse driven by bridle and whips.
He had a name that strolled in a garden
where the plants, the animals, the birds,
even the bees and wasps,

were fashioned out of gold. He had a name
that understood the book
that they held out to him
was not a mysterious object,

for they would kill him, regardless
of whether he filled the room with gold
or the riches of his being.
All that history in a name:

as if the soul of that dead Incaic emperor
could come back—would keep coming back,
again and again—
as the child of a janitor, a peasant, a clerk.

The Disbudding

A few hours after birth, the kids
butted the bottles, angrily,
                    as the fierce hunger
that made their mother's udders flow freely
collapsed the artificial
nipples.

Even then, I could feel the guilt,
as I felt the horns beginning
in the soft Alpine wool
of their crowns, the dull nubs
that would become a blinding
rack.

          I was thinking ahead, wondering whether
to circumcise my son after he was born,
trying to weigh the tenderness
of his limbs kicking within my ribs,
jubilant in the darkness of the womb,
against the historical weight
of that pruning: on the eighth day,
the infant mouth, stoppered
with a wine-soaked piece of cloth.

In the terrible repetitions of spring
          when the Lord God would circumcise
our hearts, we had to
disbud the kids early, before the armature
took root. To keep the goats from strangling,
snagged by their horns in the frame
of a fence or a feeder,
my husband and I would prune them first.
One of us would heat the iron rod
until it turned molten,
                    like the burning coal
the angel places on a stutterer's lips,
but at the touch
          of our searing ring . . .
a silent struggling in the limbs,
our voices, deliberately, counting out loud . . .
1 . . . 2 . . . 3 . . . 4 . . . 5 . . . 6 . . . 7 . . . as a fiery cloud
of steam and hair rose from a dead sea
of scorched tissue to island
each budding horn.

Painlessly

the fathers claimed: *peace*
would flow over him like a river,
no nerves in the skin of a baby or the skullcap of a goat,
but I could not believe
in their hypothetical
numbness . . . whether cradled
in ancient lambskin or strapped without
anesthesia to a modern operating table.

I had seen for myself how the horns could grow again,
       deformed by the original
burning, the tines
           twisting back into eye or brain.

Proud, rambunctious, reeking
of urine and the glory
of god, son and father of the herd, Dandylion
ripe with the scent of mating season, was meek
and stricken in our grip . . .

As the vet, removing his horns
for the second time, sliced
off the top of his skull, trying to uproot
      the veins and nerves that nurtured
the rack, made possible the crowning
              thorns,
        we kept trying to wipe the blood from our eyes,
but the buck, blinded
by blood and fear, kept tossing
his head back and forth, spattering our faces
with what none of us
could shake off, cleanse ourselves of . . .
          . . . this grasping for blessing
that is a wounding, rendering
a goat into a dying child, a child into
some god's sweet lamb, someone's baby goat . . .

Peaceable Kingdom

The lion and the lamb—no,
a pig and a coyote lie down
in the bars of my son's crib.
Each night he cuddles
the soft toy of his father's coyote,
its lupine tooth, feral ears,
a softly scowling cartoon coyote,
and a pink pig, in its velvet
coat, created in *Eden*, or
so the tag reads.

Dragging them through the carpet
or chucking their softness
into the milky hollow of his chin,
my son knows nothing of wolves feeding
upon funeral pyres or farrowing sows
that devour children who fall into
the pen, or even *this little pig*
had roast beef, this little pig had none . . .
wee, wee, crying all the way home . . .

These creatures, warm, welcoming,
fit the span of his arms.
He falls asleep, babbling,
to their unchanging expressions,
his flesh, *his flesh*, their sweet meadow.

In the Ruins

All day, I have continually thought of Astyanax.
On the front page of every newspaper, a fireman carries
the limp body of an unidentified child, as Hecuba carried
Astyanax, his eyes open as a butchered lamb's,
to bury beneath the walls of Troy. All day,
showing Euripides' *The Trojan Women*
to my freshmen English classes, the guttural cry
of Andromache has so penetrated the stone walls
that the speech teacher in the next room has trembled
outside our door, her flowered shirt beating
against the glass. Finally,
the fourth time, she burst in,
waving her arms as if swimming
toward the riveting light and, pleading
with every shrouded face, asked if
anyone could turn down the volume
so that she and her class would not be
disturbed by the "screaming on our side
of the wall." All morning, I have thought
of the children buried beneath the rubble
of the Federal Building in Oklahoma City
and have turned my face away from the crushed
Astyanax, laid out on his father's shield—his limbs and hair
like the limbs and hair of the dead child being carried away
on the front page of all the newspapers today.
Trying to glimpse the world outside
this room, its blossoming walkways, its spring
colors, through the black veil of the shutters,
all morning, I have thought of my own
son, of the milky sweetness in the hollows
of his neck, the scent of his breath, the budding
musk of his genitalia, and how that other boy
whose name meant *Lord of the City* was killed,
because, alive, he could root and flower in a field of ashes;
his living so terrified the Greeks.
All semester, I have struggled to compare
the Greek view to ours, and my students
have turned to me with the blinking gaze
of those forced to stare so long into the distance
that their eyes blur with tears. And I think Homer was wrong
when he compared the souls of the dead to a flock of bats
winging their way to the underworld,
though, when the bomb went off and so many died,

I cannot imagine what it was like, in any theology—
whether the souls were so many atoms dispersing
or a single gossamer wing. After my father died,
there were days when, suddenly, I would smell him smoking;
the phosphoric flare of a match would fill the car
as I drove to the market or past the cemetery
where the rubble of ancient graves
was scrapped in one corner of the yard, smoldering
among the leaves. The smell of that burning
clung tightly to my clothes, to the inner hairs
of my nostrils, as the stench of Troy burning
must have clung to the Greeks as they steered for home,
*the dying ashes spreading on the air the fat savour
of wealth* that Aeschylus could still smell
centuries later. I cannot imagine having to bear
my own child as that child—whose?—
is borne away in wooden arms. The souls of the dead
must be like common loons feeding on a lake.
How a single bird tips over, vanishes utterly
into the waves, its weight becoming another kind
of ripple or wake, dividing the deepest currents
with its own flesh. Not a gesture
out of, but within, the body,
wings tucked at a cutting angle, streaking
toward another silvery life. We are told
their winged forms resurface, minutes later,
on the other side of the inlet or cove,
but we cannot track that watery trajectory,
or glimpse their emergence,
their feathers, glistening as if new,
though we stand here all morning, waiting, watching.

Returning Home

I had just taken the kids
to school and, irritated, harried,
drove into the yard—not the usual
suburban lawn, but miles
of sagebrush, juniper trees, and pinon,
arid, dusty from a three-year drought.
Above the mesa, a ring of light
circled the sun, so that the sun looked
like an eyeball, only more transparent
and detached from any context
of a human face. An arc,
on either side of the sun, began dividing
the deeper blue within its curvature
from the lighter hue of the sky outside:
its pupil, the sun,
its iris, the darker surrounding blue
and for its cornea, the outer reaches
of the visible world.
As the sun burnt the fog
from the valley, I seemed to stare
into a giant eye that hovered
over the rim of the earth.
In the legend that Ueshiba
made of his life, as a young man
in a Japanese village, swearing to conquer
the political thugs who routinely beat his father,
he apprenticed himself to any stronger
master: death, the army, the war.
Years later, his father long dead,
himself his father's age, he created
aikido, "way of love," when a halo
rose in his garden—not down
from heaven, but out of the earth.
As the eye, that heavenly glare
began to break apart, I saw the air was full
of ice crystals—their rising had created the view—
each tiny sliver, drifting, dispersing, melting away
into the world, its light.

Boy With Snake

As beautiful as any Roman infant
carved of marble, the flawless flex
of his feet and arms, the curly locks
that have not yet been cut, my son grasps
at whatever moves, rushes to savor
whatever falls within reach: a scrap of paper,
a piece of lint on the living room carpet,
as enticing as a cherry, a plum
of untranslated sweetness.

As always, the snake is danger's
facsimile, this time, molded
of dimestore rubber, a cobra blind
in its eyeless hood, crude markings
of a second poisonous face, spray-painted
on the back of its head which is always turned
toward paradise, the hushed leaves,
the motionless planets,
poised on a burning branch.

If I find its ten feet of threat
coiled on the bathroom tile or jammed
behind the sauna door, I recoil a moment,
automatically, taught to shudder,
by history—my own and others'—
at a snake's dark inverted diamonds,
the slack heft of its earthen tongue.
This morning as my son scuttles
across the carpet, I let the snake fall
within his reach. He crawls

toward it as gladly
as he does to whatever's new,
the knot of the world uncoiling
at his tiny wedge-shaped feet.
He wrestles that blind gaze
up to his face, for he knows
by smelling and by taste:
fits to his own mouth, that other
tongue of Eden, its split red fork.

Eating of the Tree of Life

on our seventeenth anniversary,

Years ago, when I made you that poster,
that collage of photographs snipped
from magazines, the flora and fauna
of the world, it was the symmetrical
resonance between the sleeping ibis, its beak
folded into its thick neck feathers,
and the heron raising its head to the sky
as if it could drink that blue, or the way
the curve of the seashell replicated
the whorl of a cloud, that appealed,
every gesture answering or opposed.
Two moose were swimming across
the glacial blue of a Montana lake,
their antlered heads crowning the waters,
while, further down, in their Africa,
the spotted necks of two young deer
in an X, as they extended soft snouts
to one another. The twos, all the duos,
matched or asymmetrical pairs. But now I see
preserved beneath the lacquer—the reflective
sheen taking on an opaque body of its own,
its skin translucent as honey or amber—our
entire lives transpiring into another, as the curve
of an eagle's wing, soaring in a corner, becomes
earthbound, burdened, in the straining
arch of a donkey's neck, then rises, again,
into the nearly transparent wing of a bee,
working rapidly from flower to flower. All we
know of beauty is the necessity that breaks
and uplifts the continents into these
alpine views, the drag of the moon that sculpts
the coastline while ravaging the small, fertile
tidal pools, the wind that erodes a mountain
with a river of green rain, all this
grace of mountain or desert or swamp
originating in the draft and drift
that drew us to one another, impelled
by the same force. Like the cross
in the center of the poster, whose limbs
are the microscopic color photographs
of molecular structures, cells or chemical compounds,
we are, and are not, our aggregations.

How could I know then, how could you,
that the soft muzzling motion of the animals
was another dance that would wheel us
constantly out of ourselves, and into another?
We began as the only two human figures
in this scene, the only two in black and white
among the spotted and speckled. There
at the base of the poster, as if the cross
and its towering tree of life were rooted
in their spines, two Peruvian children,
a boy and a girl, lean insolently
on either side of a round table that
their arms reach across, their hands
entwining almost casually at its edge.
As if they with the soft, bruised
hats of their people and their patched
Sunday best knew all along, knew
from the beginning, of that house
at the center of the world,
where the faces of children drift
like seeds, and everyone must
go down, dancing.

The Scent of the Skin

When to the rhythm
of my husband's snore, my son cocks
his two-year-old leg over
his father's hip, snuggles

deep into that parental rib,
I lean over and without touching—
my nostrils poised at the brink
of his curls—breathe in

the baby scent of him. Beneath the common
smell of soap, Mickey Mouse pajamas,
there is another scent—
indescribable, *him*,

a boyish musk, that I bend to
as he all summer knelt to the unfolding of
the roses, nosing the petals with his eyes, opening
his mouth to their colors.

Each of my children inhaled the world like this,
Maria cuddling my pillow said it smelled
of frankincense,
Ann put on her father's shirt

as if it were his dark, rich skin,
while I, sniffing, could smell nothing,
from years of letting the world go up
in smoke. How transitory

it is, how brief. So I lie here,
just breathing, trying to stay
awake forever in the garden
of this bed.

To the Muses

                        Scarred by those
who conquered the mountain
and carved their victory in your bark,
the lovers who hoped to twine forever
in your groves, the wanderers
who gouged the date of their passing,
a black scribble blighting you
with our desire to be
remembered,
                your forms,
white-trunked, slim, became
the forest of our words, the leaves
of our pages turning in the wind, the myths
of our enchanted minds, until we could scarcely tell
you from ourselves or scan the meaning
of what we had written . . .

                        You have lived so long at those elevations
where we imagined you, lofty and airless.
Transplant yourselves among us.
Your mother, it is said, was memory.
Reawaken in us the longing when, within the earth,
thirst and tenderness began to knit one desolation
to another, filling each vacancy
with a green, a fruitful shape.

                        Once I saw a guard outside a music tent,
a man who had silenced a crowd successfully
so that the music, clear, limpid, could drift
across the lawn, turn red with frustration
at the rising, unmeasured singing
of the aspen trees . . .

                        Speak to us
with that other voice, multifarious,
ordinary, sweet.

In the Shadow of Chronos

It's a child's toy that I kick up, aimlessly
waiting for my friend to cross the threshold,
her eyes, *ojerosa,* blinking against the last
flare of the sun's torch. Unearthed
in her back yard, this terrible tiny figure
startles, as if it were that zodiacal creature
Goethe spoke of, child of the *telluric*
planet, Saturn . . . that strong worldiness
which clings . . . to the earth: half-woman,
half-serpent, breasts swollen as if
she had just given birth, but without
nipples, unable to suckle,
the red crest of hair swept upward
in the rigid shape of a helmet,
its thought, a winged weapon of war,
its stare, the *daemonic*
gaze of nature.

Every afternoon, my friend struggles
to speak as chronic fatigue *holds sway*
over the summer lake of her face,
each syllable falling like a stone
into *the dead plane of the mirroring*
surface, I sought to save myself
from this terrible being.
She tries to locate the origins
of her illness by describing
the spasms forking into her skeletal frame.
How she wastes away, her bed
a dark, dank, meadow of the underworld
where she lies in the limbo of flowers,
neither living nor dead but still
attached to a crushed stem, and dreams
and dreams and dreams and dreams of crawling
out of the grass.

I've seen the figure before,
on a "storycloth" embroidered
by the Hmong of Vietnam,
a flower cloth sent by another
friend, *no longer the goddess*
whom you lost, yet it is divine,
yet that half woman, half fish

is the only human, the only solo
in a colorful landscape of animal pairs:
two wild deer in dark and light russet,
two blue peacocks, two boars in contrary green.
Floating in a small lake, she feeds lotus blossoms
to two dragons, and the crowning flames
of the dragons' crests are the fiery shape
of the lotus bloom: as if what consumes
and is consumed, like the two leaves
floating on the surface of the pool, bear
the singular shape of the human heart.

In that other version of paradise,
the tree of life and the tree of knowledge
are threaded in common ground,
but in the distortions of this cheap toy,
made by those silenced and starving
in factory prisons, only the fear
of the mythic lingers,
this *tender, hideous sea-nixie,*
so potent, it drags memory
in its wake, dredging up those depths
where the half-forgotten and the never-were
mix and mingle in the nets of blame.
I wonder if on our last visit, my children
found the toy and buried it again, so
they wouldn't have to look at those breasts,
or did I stub back into the ground
that mouth's shrieking O?

I don't know what to do, fear leaving it
like a small corpse, a grave full of bad luck
on the perimeter of my friend's life.
As my friend emerges, I tell of the accidental
unearthing, place the object in her palm.
She grimaces and flings it into a wastebin
where it will wait for months to be discarded
like some ancient, unacknowledged guilt.
And when I find the figure, months later,
in an advertisement for the *Return
of the Monster Women,* one of several
half women, half snake or lizard or cat,
from a replica of a 1950's lunchpail,
nothing will be solved.

I will keep thinking of it, haunted
as if it were the riddle
of my friend's illness, preferring
to believe the figure is like those Jerusalem
crickets that with their huge heads
and translucent forms haunt my garden.
Children of the earth, the old people
call those nocturnal messengers
which I usually find floating
in the pond among the water lilies,
their flesh already beginning to dissolve
between one realm and the next.
Only once have I seen one, alive,
in sunlight, its strange beauty emerging
from the earth, like Inanna returning
from the underworld where she hung,
flesh rotting, as she sang and sang and sang
and sang until she died.

                    Cradled momentarily
in the sunlight of my hand,
the cricket mewed like a baby;
when I let it go, it went singing,
bearing the weight of that almost human head,
that almost divine gaze, into the valley
of the shadow of death.

Hymn to Aphrodite

An iron wing descends within you, dividing
you from yourself. In the sea,
among the living tendrils of the grass,
the tiny pipe of Priapus,

the seahorse, floats sadly, knowing
it will be caught in the nets,
bridled and noosed, left
to die slowly, its flesh drying

into a dusty potion to restore,
supposedly, the flagged desire
of aged men. But the stolen horns
of the rhinoceros, the crushed

skull of the tiger, the seas
empty of the hippocampus, do not testify
to the power and cruelty of Aphrodite.
She was lost before we lost her.

Once, she was a goddess of war. If
you shook your fist at her, she would bite it,
leaving your flesh, torn and inflamed
with the arc of her perfect teeth.

It was said that the fever
would enter the very marrow of your spine,
and in the delirium of your burning,
you could hear her singing

outside the temple.
There was no darkness within her body,
a cloud banking through unkempt waters,
she illuminated the fields.

She fled shimmering from the battlefield
where she kept being wounded, seized
by something like love. In Palestine,
the tomb of Christ was built upon a ruined

temple of Aphrodite: there, the snow keeps falling
and falling, like snow,
not bread,
from the sky.

The Book Breaks Open

On Easter as the readings wind their way toward the
        resurrection,
I am aware of how every story erases, ignores,
the body of the woman; not one page acknowledges
the thick fibers of the uterus,
or trumpets the unfurling Fallopian tube, or heralds
the womb's expelling urgency or echoes
that groan of triumph. These tales,

each one licked at the edges
with gold leaf, always end

with a dividing sword, and the words
spoken by God Himself
are written in blood red letters,
like the thin red trickle of ribbon
with which the priest keeps
his place and to which the pages always fall
open. The script acknowledges nothing,

except *mother*, dim memory of a breast engorged
by generosity and restraint.

Dividing us, dividing the sea 'red'
with unbelieving blood, the priest admonishes
us to be the beloved, to follow that consuming
fire down the muddy corridor
where the waters upon which spirit of God danced
solidify into opaque walls—
rather than that one

who dives into openness,
and drowns.

The altar boys, struggling under the weight
of the book, try to remain as motionless
as the limp, docile pages that do not
rise in the breeze that rushes
through the windows. Held down
by the number of its pages, the weight of its binding,
prone on its spine, the book splits open
upon the altar, is

anointed
with incense, blessed before any

of the human forms, exhaling, inhaling,
hushed, attendant upon the book.
Among so many others, suddenly,
I am thinking of you,
how in the hallway, your body
flooded my mind with the flowering
scent of the purple-lipped,
fringed, riot of orchid,
that I buried my face

in in
a garden once

in Florida. Rooted
in knots or where the branches joined
the trunks, the orchids thrived
on the surplus rain that ran down
the length of each tree and pooled
at its junctures, each blossom, taking nothing
from the tree, but only an anchor,
an intersection.

So your body inter-
sects the idea of the body, brings back

what I have exiled, banished,
to mere calves, breasts, eyes, thighs, recitations
of anatomy and appetite, rebukes
me with your brown
and peach, sweet
drench of wine. How the scent

reaches beyond
the scent of this

frankincense
with which the priest censors
the air. Now as we struggle
to get up from where we have been
kneeling for so long, folding and unfolding our hands
in pleas, or bent in the poses
of boredom and politeness, what raises
us, in each of us, *is* us,
the undeniable other,

holy, and still driven out
of the pages of the book.

Almost Grown

Each morning, transporting
the bass-viol, I wrap my arms
around its waist
and use my back to lift
its shrouded weight into the car,
or waddle its expectant emptiness
into the music room. Its wooden form
thumps against my thighs and knees,
as awkward in my arms
as my daughter, at times, elbowing
her way into stubborn adolescence.
This morning, in a hurry, I jerked it up
from the floor, and the scroll,
flying up, clipped the side of my forehead;
all day, my temple twanged
to the overly tightened string
of that curved vase of silence. Its almost
feminine shape resonates, caught
on a door frame or step, ringing out
at my every slip, so I lug it from room to room
as carefully as once I cradled
my daughter, a drowsy infant,
toward her crib. I know I will never make
this instrument sing, that the sheathed bow
quivering at its side is time's arrow
that flies in only one direction,
though it is still now, waiting
to be released as the music is
released. When my daughter
stands the bass up, it is almost a living
being, leaning against her,
and as she begins to play,
her arm slowly drawing or plucking
the sweetness out of it,
the sound flows through the floors
of the house, into the foundation, up through
the soles of our feet, pouring
into our ears, the pores
of our skin. That dark music,
that honeyed tone echoes
my own loss and longing;
it's the voice of *her* life,
as familiar and new as her own body
beginning to change.

How to Speak In Babylon

Breathe. Bow once in the direction
of death. Open your hand
like the fist of the newly born.
Nod toward the couple
married for fifty years
who are still dancing the two-step beneath
the bright heaven they have made
of temporarily buoyant balloons. Grip
your fear as carefully
as you would hold a bee
between your fingers, wanting
neither to crush it
or to be stung. Speak
and remember the cord
still knotted invisibly
around your throat.
In the corner, a woman is
talking to some strangers,
and at your nod, her face
flushes with something
like love, her hand
rises, her palm pressed
in the space between her breasts,
as if the word flew, there,
into her heart. But though
the gesture moves you,
you are not speaking for her,
but for that heavenly emptiness
that gathers beneath her wings
all the sorrows of this
Jerusalem. Recall
that moment when your life
knotted in your throat
before the empty church,
the miles of vacant pews,
and how you launched
your voice out, for nothing,
for no one, into that nothingness,
knowing you would be able to do this,
open your lips and speak . . .

Every Scrap of Paper

Hoarding every fragment,
believing that *amatl* wedded
the natural world and the human word
into an eternal thing, the Aztecs
adorned with paper

those who were to be sacrificed:
slaves waving paper flags, maidens
crowned with paper, children wrapped in paper
as offerings for the gods. One word,

written on paper made from the serpent tree,
defined the stars and the living calendar,
bound the villagers and the dead who slept
beneath the floor. It took centuries

to make paper, the inner fibers
stripped from the great fig tree,
drowned in water, dried, then boiled,
finally burnished by stones

to close the pores, centuries
to envelope the human form
with another skin, blank, unblemished,
on which could be written

signs to control the world.
As a child, flaying
the skin from a birch,
over and over again, I tried writing

with a sharp stick on the speckled
underside, smudging on the pelt
of that stubborn species.
Frayed by my knife, gaping

where the knots would not relinquish
their hold but left the wounds
of their tearing away, the pages
never looked like paper
but flesh torn from a tree.

The Kingdom of Fear

For Ruth Stone

I don't want to die—no; I neither want to die nor do I want to want to die. I want to live forever and ever and ever. I want this "I" to live this poor "I . . . "

Miguel de Unamuno

I knew there was no help for it
when I forgot my daughter's paper
for the international competition—in triplicate,
collated graphs, decimals and English proofread
by six judges—on the roof of the Jeep as I wrestled
the baby into his car seat, though I still let out
a howl when turning around to retrieve what I had lost,
I rounded a curve into a blizzard, those pages

now a white whirlwind in the juniper trees.
I knew there was no help for it
when I told my father out in the pasture
that my first poem had been accepted and, flinty-mouthed,
up to his knees in muck, he turned and said, *yes,
you'll be famous and I'll be hanging from a tree.*
I knew there was no help for it when I found Toni,
our white-necked Alpine doe, her throat torn out,

in the furthest, darkest, corner of her pen,
where she'd put her back to the wall for shelter,
nor for the neighbor's dog whose dragging chain
I tracked up the sandy arroyo. They'd chained
the bloody animal to the porch as if it had come home,
wagging its tail, any dog on any day. Though I could sue,
have the cur destroyed, collect $782 in small claims,
there was no help for Toni, her elegant stroll

to the milking stand, her sweet gallon a day;
for eight years, I'd kept her out of the herds
driven to slaughter or to market, precisely
so she would never die like that. No help for it,
every spring, when I'd lift the hammer and bring it down
upon the skull of another struggling kid goat,
thinking mercy was this gesture of knocking it out
before cutting its throat. No help for the axe

fallen from my hand, the buckets of water frozen solid
before the thirsty flocks. The water would flow again, but not
according to my need; many I loved would be borne away
by the current, and, waiting for my son to be born,
I would wake at night, terrified of how I would be torn
and pried apart, until, one night, I stared into a gaze
without eyes—a black, imperial, visage
that looked and looked and said nothing.

I knew there was no help for it, in the dead of winter,
when, as a child walking through a cemetery,
I jumped into an empty grave. I sat at the bottom
of the cold, staring into the blank blue eye
that hovered above and saw, in the frozen flanks of the earth,
the sheered roots of neighboring trees, their white grasp
at an end. My fear kicking a handhold,
I barely scrambled out. I knew then,

that was the beginning . . . I felt something moving,
rising like music emerging from a fretted neck, or water
cascading over a precipice that it simultaneously erodes—
the black veils lifting against the updraft of the falls.
It was the dark dance in the *Popol Vuh* when the twins, killed
by the Lords of Death, their bones ground into the river,
come back as catfish, vagabonds, as ragged men dancing
the Armadillo, the Dance of the Poorwill,

one of them dying for the other, Xbalanque spreading wide
the arms of Little Hunahpu, his head rolling away,
his heart smothered in a leaf, sacrificing each other
and bringing each other back to life, springing up
like the corn stalks from which their flesh was formed,
until dying seems painless, almost a dance.
The Lords of Death groaned with longing to rise
and fall in that sweet jumble of limbs,

those jaguar-mawed, canine-snouted Lords broken
by the desire to live and die, to be caught
as we are caught up. It was the same song I would hear
crackling on a recording from the 1930's, Heifitz
playing the dawning end of his world, the song of the soul
crawling out of the underworld, *I* like a melody
unraveling out of static, out of
the white noise of the primordial void.

Heart's Chord

Two frozen levels beneath us, the landlord
had pitched a sound system on his roof
to broadcast Christmas carols
to the trailer park; his house,
the only one built of stone, was the hub
that anchored circle after circle
of shiny rectangles, metal roofs, radiating
up the terraced Vermont hill. The stream
that divided the upper and lower levels
was not yet iced over; I could hear it chugging
over the rocks, its murmur, continuous,
subterranean, beneath the brass instruments
halleujahing a temporary *Joy to the World*.
As I trudged back and forth in my subzero
refusal to go back home, my boots
broke through the crust and began
filling with snow. *Peace on earth*,
but I could only feel the stinging:
that afternoon, my friend
had put rocks and rimes of ice
in the center of the snowballs
she made for the endless volley
which drove me, eyes weeping involuntarily,
up the frozen hill, home
to where my parents were smoldering,
their anger with one another
like piles of dead, damp, leaves
that could only dream of conflagration.
In school, we had scissored
snowflakes out of construction paper;
hung in the hall, the unmelting shapes
were meant to illustrate our uniqueness:
each one, the only one in eternity's drift.
I could not believe it. It would take a moment,
decades later, in a blinding snowstorm,
beneath an oak tree, beyond all seeming,
its branches, a galaxy rooted
on the side of a hill, to forgive
what fell from heaven, to feel that drift
as any kind of blessing,
melting on my eyes and tongue.

Ginevra d'Benci

Everywhere, the same relentless movement:
words clouding at the edge of disorder, a small block

of row houses lining up, for decades
the concrete permeated with the scent of our passing,

acrid with rain, tears, sweat, the same scent
that in the desert smells sweet, as passing by,

a person brushes against a plant or crushes
a branch underfoot, and the bruising itself

brings forth the oil, the holy scent. In the desert,
the juniper in its wrinkled fronds, grips a decade of dust,

and the blue perfect spheres of its berries are bitter,
consumed by nothing, not even the birds of the air.

For the desert is the city's end . . . Exhuming the great ruins,
the shovels bite into the red substrata, unearthing:

beads like a galaxy of tiny apple seeds from a consumed core,
a vanished finding, indigestible kernels

of 8-row and 10-row corn, a brush of human hair,
the disarticulated skeletons of six captive

children, a coracoid of a duck, a single horned lark,
the shriveled remains of an uneaten frog,

perhaps, used for ceremonial purposes, the handle
of a broken pot, an offering for the infant interred

in a trash heap. As the junipers are forever contracted
in their wooden rings to ancient decades of drought,

so the femurs of the children bear as many as seven lines
of arrested growth, lines that mark the times

when due to disease, starvation, they abruptly stopped growing.
Such tiny and bitter seeds, cut off forever

from the land of the living, such a crop of resentment
hoarded in some pack rat's den, the golden measure

slowly hardening into a stone-like semblance.
For the excavation *Peeling back, one by one,*

the eluding surfaces is like the attempted
unveiling of Draupadi in the Mahabarata,

how the Lords gambled to strip away the single garment
that she wore. But as one corner of her robe

was torn away, another fold enveloped her. Unraveling
her clothing was unraveling the seam

of existence itself, the radiant fabric accumulating in drifts.
Draupadi had five husbands and in the year that she spent

with each one, the other four swore not
to try and embrace her, even in their minds,

but who can bear that unending river, the weight of endlessness,
that garment drifting across the sky?

For the city is the desert's beginning, there
in the nation's capital, I have seen the drift

in the residue of brick, the snow of concrete,
and on its branches, the juniper berry of a human

face, a portrait of Ginevra d'Benci, a white oval,
an acrid turn at the corner of her lip denying

the sweet modulations of her skin, for the tree
which never overwhelms her with its dark multiplications

is meant as a sign and an emblem
of her character. She stands within that juniper tree,

as if the human face, the human form were the final fruit
of those branches: its needles exacting

a mathematical screen, so painfully wrought,
it seems the very net, the very end

of human desire.

Mother Tongue

So here I am again thinking of you—
out in the garden, sweeping up
the pink scentless clusters of the bougainvillea,
torn apart by an unexpected cold spell.
Behind the heavy clay pots of the jades,
their succulent leaves like fat thumbs cocked
at the sun, I find the forgotten
maidenhair fern—what is left of it, shoved
so long ago into the shade to recover—
its stems, wires of shorn hair
bristling out of a black mound
of root and soil. I don't know
if it's alive and dormant, if
it will ever thrive. I could blame
the aridity of this climate, but, you know,
even in humid Wisconsin, years ago, I couldn't
revive the two you asked me to keep. "Maidenhair,"
"Venus hair", they call the delicate fronds
like the hair of the goddess rising
out of the damp shadows of a forest,
or the scalloped edges of a mountain stream.
The last time I saw them growing in the wild,
was in Arizona, at Montezuma's Well,
a spring as round as a blue eye, enormous,
sunk into stone, thousands of gallons of water streaming
out of the desert rock, fluid mother
tongue. Only soft-shelled turtles
and a unique species of microscopic life
could inhabit the unusual acidity
of the water, and—where a prehistoric people
had carved a ditch at the base of a cliff, directing
the earth's outpouring toward their small patches
of pumpkins and corn—the maidenhair ferns
luxuriantly, shading the hacked, hewn channels.
I thought of your hair—that striking mane,
and that delicate thatch of a deeper, more intimate, color
like the maidenhair fern, *mons veneris*, softly
swelling above the pubic bone.

Fear Is the Mother of the Mind

We were killing time in Valencia,
waiting for the door of the Apostles to open
and allow us a glimpse of the Holy Grail,
as if then we would taste the vanished wine.

But it was siesta, the cathedral
and the adjoining Our Lady of the Forsaken were closed,
so we kept circling the Plaza like sleepwalkers
as the stones moaned beneath our feet.

It seemed the ground itself was feverish,
dreaming of some historical nightmare,
an ancient *auto-de-fe* or the feast
of St. Joseph, when every spring

the cardboard Lords of the Earth
are blown apart, fireworks planted
into their bellies, their flesh—
the *fallas,* the city's confetti.

As we circled the church, a man
with a terrifying scar that crisscrossed
his shaved head, began shadowing us,
abruptly turning to shout *Shut Up!*

at something invisible that dogged
his elbow, or else, quieted,
no longer plagued, turned
to stare at our children

with the more alarming rapture
of an instant angel. We kept retreating
to the center of the Plaza,
for he seemed to fear the fountain

where a white marble Poseidon,
lounging on his side amid a dozen nymphs,
was surrounded by a hedge of lances,
an iron ring of bars.

The water streaming out of the nymphs
anointed only the gigantic god himself,
casting no coolness in our direction,
burning up in the Levantine sun.

A few steps away, a small fountain
stood in the shade. A slab of stone,
the size of an average man's tombstone,
bore an inscription and a spigot

with the bronze head
of a Medusa. At a turn of a hand,
a trickle flowed out of her mouth
into a dirty basin below.

All through Europe, I'd seen her
on palatial entrances, grimacing
in official seals, sometimes disguised
by the flatulent curls of the sun king,

sometimes sketched crudely in dolomite,
quarried from a prehistoric cave.
More than once, bending to drink
or marvel at the marble disk of a fountain,

I'd been startled by her eyes staring
up through the effervescence, her face
carved into the depths, water spouting
from the O of her mouth,

her utterance, a watery chaos
that flooded and filled the eyes, the voice
of the wounded other
flowing out of an unstoppable wound.

Incredible,
the myth embodied so,
her small tomb so near to the god
who'd raped her, so long ago,

in the temple of wisdom,
her face becoming a bronze seal
of horror, her lips still straining
to give birth.

When the church finally opened
its heavy doors, and we crossed the portal
of every Thursday, and were swallowed
into the dim, exhausted, interior,

I couldn't believe that Christ
had ever touched that cup.
It seemed more plunder
than pilgrimage. Its golden rim

meant for the glazed stare
of the display, like the arm
of St. Vincent in the next chapel,
his entire arm from the elbow down

arranged upon a pillow, to extend
his hand, its precious stones
toward an imaginary kiss.
In this city of his martyrdom—

starved in prison, pierced,
burnt on a grille, disemboweled,
his arms torn out
in opposite directions—

he himself must have longed
for mercy, the angels
tearing out their wings
to feather the floor of his cell.

Incredible, to see
belief embodied so,
the foundlings
singing, the lunatics rapt,

as the statue of the Virgin of the Forsaken
was carried into the chapel,
upon the coffin of one
who died, abandoned, unknown.

We could not leave quickly enough,
that city of the Grail, the lost
still gathering in its streets, the gods
lounging in the square,

and, as we raced toward our car,
we passed again the Medusa fountain
where an emaciated dog, standing
on the rim, was licking up

the few, remaining drops.
Since then, I've wished many times
that I'd stopped a moment, pressed my lips
to hers, had the nerve to plunge

my face and hands into those waters
thriving with multitudes and microbes.

Mythos

When we returned home, it was
the body of the earth
that greeted us, the air
thick with the scent of those
dusty, arid flanks,
the scent of the ashes
in our own bones flowering
in the fronds of the juniper,
the depths of the rabbitbrush.
Coming back from the rush and road
of concrete canyons, the scent
of exhaust and gasoline rising
from the sidewalks and the walls,
it was like flowering oneself,
in the cells of one's body, to breathe in—
nostrils flaring, mouth inhaling—
the scent of the earth and what grew
upon it, a body of infinite form, one limb
curving into the other, and the air
like the breath transpiring from its languid lips.
I felt like a child again, when, driven
out of the house by sadness, the piercing
cry of the meadowlarks spaced
in their kingdoms of the air, perched
along the crests of the telephone poles
calling me further and further into the distance,
I would fling myself upon the ground
and lie upon the earth, my arms outspread
as if crucified. But I was not
crucified; I was one diving
face downward into the earth, feeling
the pull upon my atoms and cells, calling
me back into the dust, the same dust
that the Milky Way scattered, shivering
open the sky at night, the seeds of
winnowing, the ashes of harvest.
As I lay there, I was comforted,
the earth itself became my mother,
and then, by turns, a father,
a friend, a lover, and in each of those moments,
as I lay upon the ground, I held out
my hands in a sign of great emptiness,
for I could not grasp or span that living form

but could only float upon it
as the leaves of the water lilies
float on the surface of the water,
holding themselves millimeters above
the rippling, in broad palms
of green. And in the infinite whispering,
the click of crickets caught in the grass,
the shifting labor of the ants,
I would hear, not the ancient
voice of some muttering god,
but the hum of the earth itself.

Notes:

I am told that the poem on the dedication page by my father was published in the Concord, Massachusetts, newspaper, sometime in 1951, and that it was his only publication.

"27 November 1992"—on this date, a student in Venezuela was murdered, apparently, for no more than being a student. His name was Atahualpa Perez. Atahualpa was the name of the Inca at the time of the conquest by Pizarro and the poem refers to various events in his life: how Pizarro charged at him on horseback and was astonished when he stood his ground, and how the priests were surprised that Atahualpa was not afraid of a book, the Bible with which they approached him. The garden where even the insects were fashioned out of gold was found in Cuzco.

I am indebted to Eleanor Wilner for the observation of the evolution of the crescent in "Original Darkness" and the title of "Welcome to Ithaca," as well as for several suggestions and hesitations.

The quotes in "In the Shadow of Chronos" are taken from Walter Benjamin's "Goethe's Elective Affinities."

In "The Disbudding" the quote "may peace flow over you like a river" is from "Song for Circumsion" by Shalem Shabazi, translated by T. Carmi in *The Penguin Book of Hebrew Poets*.

In "The Harrowing" "a terrible deity, a human scalp in one hand, / in the other, a seashell, / full of blood" is a pastiche from the *Tibetan Book of the Dead*.

In "Ginevra d'Benci" "Peeling back, /one by one, the eluding / surfaces" is a quote from Walter Benjamin.

Biographical Note

Rebecca Seiferle has previously published two books with Sheep Meadow, *The Ripped-Out Seam* and a translation of César Vallejo's *Trilce*. She received an external degree from the University of the State of New York with a major in English and History, and a minor in Art History. In 1989 she received an MFA from Warren Wilson College. Seiferle teaches English and creative writing at San Juan Community College. She lives in Farmington, New Mexico with her husband and three children.